The Heroic Legacy of the 6888th Battalion

How Major Charity Adams and the Six Triple Eight Overcame Racism, Misogyny, and War

TIFFANY C. KINGSBURY

COPYRIGHT

TABLE OF CONTENTS

INTRODUCTION

The Unsung Heroes of World War II

World War II is often remembered for its towering figures, massive battles, and pivotal turning points, but beneath the surface lies an array of untold stories of heroism and resilience. Among these are the contributions of the 6888th Central Postal Directory Battalion, an all-Black, all-female unit whose work not only boosted the morale of millions of soldiers but also shattered deeply entrenched racial and gender barriers.

Nicknamed the "Six Triple Eight," the battalion faced a monumental task: clearing a mail backlog of over 17 million letters and packages for American soldiers stationed in

The Heroic Legacy of the 6888th Battalion

Europe. At a time when communication was the lifeline for troops far from home, their work was indispensable. Despite the overwhelming scale of their mission, the women of the 6888th accomplished their goal with remarkable efficiency, all while battling prejudice, harsh working conditions, and the realities of war.

Their achievements went largely unheralded in their time, overshadowed by the broader narratives of the war and the prevailing racial and gender inequities of mid-20th-century America. Yet their story remains one of extraordinary courage, determination, and perseverance—a testament to the unsung heroes who played a pivotal role in shaping the outcome of history.

The Importance of Telling the 6888th's Story

For decades, the story of the Six Triple Eight was relegated to the margins of history books, a footnote in the grand narrative of World War II. This erasure not only did a disservice to the women who served but also to the broader understanding of the war effort and the progress it inspired.

The 6888th's story underscores the intersection of race, gender, and service in a segregated military, highlighting how African American women navigated dual forms of discrimination to make meaningful contributions.

It also challenges the traditional image of a soldier, broadening the definition of service to include those who worked behind the scenes to sustain the morale and welfare of the troops.

In an era when representation matters more than ever, revisiting and amplifying the achievements of the Six Triple Eight is both a moral imperative and an opportunity to inspire future generations. Their story provides a blueprint for resilience in the face of adversity, demonstrating how courage and determination can break down barriers and leave an indelible mark on history.

A Legacy Rediscovered

The rediscovery of the 6888th Battalion's legacy is a testament to the power of storytelling and the importance of preserving history. For nearly 80 years, their contributions were overlooked, their names forgotten, and their achievements unsung. It wasn't until the 21st century that their story began to emerge from the shadows, culminating in a Congressional Medal of Honor awarded to the unit in 2022.

The resurgence of interest in their story can be credited to historians, advocates, and cultural creators who recognized the significance of their contributions. Tyler Perry's The Six Triple Eight brings their legacy to a global audience, ensuring that their heroism is not just remembered but celebrated.

As the last living members of the 6888th Battalion approach the end of their lives, the urgency to honor their contributions grows. This renewed focus on their story offers a chance to not only rectify historical omissions but also to inspire a new generation with their example of service, unity, and perseverance.

The Six Triple Eight's journey from obscurity to recognition serves as a reminder that history is never static—it evolves with the voices we choose to amplify. Their legacy, once forgotten, is now a powerful beacon, shining a light on the enduring contributions of African American women in the fight for equality and justice, both at home and abroad.

CHAPTER ONE

Breaking Barriers in Uniform

The journey to inclusivity and equality within the U.S. military was neither swift nor easy. It was marked by significant milestones, hard-fought battles, and trailblazers who defied societal norms to create opportunities for future generations. The creation of the Women's Army Corps (WAC) and the rise of figures like Charity Adams symbolize the breaking of barriers in uniform, laying the foundation for the contributions of the 6888th Battalion.

The Road to Women in the Military

Before World War II, women's roles in the military were minimal, often restricted to nursing or administrative positions. The idea of women in uniform serving in a combat-adjacent capacity was viewed with skepticism and resistance. However, the onset of global conflict in 1939 and America's entry into the war in 1941 dramatically shifted this perspective.

The attack on Pearl Harbor and the ensuing mobilization for World War II created an urgent need for manpower. With millions of men enlisting or being drafted, the military faced severe labor shortages. To address this, leaders began to consider incorporating women into the armed forces in non-combat roles, enabling more men to serve on the front lines.

Resistance to this idea was widespread. Critics argued that women lacked the physical and mental toughness required for military life, while others feared the potential breakdown of traditional gender roles. Additionally, racial segregation and discrimination compounded these challenges for African American women, who faced systemic barriers even as they sought to serve their country.

Despite these obstacles, the need for a larger workforce eventually prevailed over societal biases. Women began to take on roles traditionally reserved for men, proving their capability and challenging preconceived notions about gender.

Formation of the Women's Army Corps (WAC)

The establishment of the Women's Army Auxiliary Corps (WAAC) on May 14, 1942, marked a turning point in military history. Signed into law by President Franklin D. Roosevelt, this legislation allowed women to serve in the Army for the first time, though initially in an auxiliary capacity. Women in the WAAC were not considered part of the regular Army and lacked many of the rights and privileges afforded to male soldiers.

The WAAC program attracted thousands of women eager to contribute to the war effort, but its auxiliary status quickly proved problematic. Recognizing the need for a more robust integration of women into the military, Congress passed legislation in 1943 converting the WAAC into the Women's Army Corps (WAC), granting women full military status.

The WAC opened doors for women to serve in a variety of roles, from clerks and mechanics to radio operators and postal workers. However, the military's policies reflected the racial inequalities of the time. African American women were admitted to the WAC but faced segregation and limited opportunities compared to their white counterparts.

Despite these challenges, the WAC became a crucial component of the U.S. war effort. By the end of the war, over 150,000 women had served in the WAC, proving their value to the military and paving the way for future generations.

Charity Adams: A Trailblazing Leader

Charity Adams' journey to becoming the first African American woman commissioned as an officer in the Women's Army Corps is a story of ambition, resilience, and leadership. Born in 1918 in Columbia, South Carolina, Adams grew up in a family that valued education and service. Her parents instilled in her a sense of purpose and the belief that she could achieve greatness, even in a world that often sought to limit her potential.

In 1942, Adams was teaching junior high math and science when she received an invitation to apply for the WAAC. Intrigued by the opportunity to serve her country and develop her leadership skills, she accepted. After completing rigorous officer candidate training, she earned her commission and quickly distinguished herself as a capable and inspiring leader.

Adams' rise through the ranks was not without challenges. As one of the few Black women in a predominantly white institution, she faced prejudice and skepticism. Yet she remained undeterred, focusing on her mission and the well-being of the women under her command.

Her leadership came to define the 6888th Battalion. Under her guidance, the Six Triple Eight tackled the monumental task of clearing the mail backlog in Europe, an achievement that demonstrated the strength and capability of women of color in the military. Adams' ability to navigate the intersecting challenges of racism, sexism, and war earned her respect and admiration, both within the Army and beyond.

Charity Adams' legacy is not only one of personal accomplishment but also of systemic change. Her success opened doors for countless women who followed in her footsteps, proving that excellence knows no bounds of race or gender. As the commanding officer of the 6888th Battalion, she exemplified the values of courage, perseverance, and leadership, becoming a trailblazer whose impact continues to resonate today.

CHAPTER TWO

Building the 6888th Battalion

The formation of the 6888th Central Postal Directory Battalion marked a significant milestone in American military history. It was the first and only all-Black, all-female battalion deployed overseas during World War II, created to address a critical logistical challenge while showcasing the potential of African American women in uniform.

The journey to building this historic unit was filled with challenges, but the women of the Six Triple Eight proved their mettle, uniting in diversity and overcoming systemic discrimination to become an integral part of the U.S. Army's war effort.

The Heroic Legacy of the 6888th Battalion

The Call to Serve

As the United States ramped up its involvement in World War II, the demand for efficient communication became paramount. Letters and packages served as lifelines for soldiers stationed overseas, providing a critical morale boost during a grueling and uncertain conflict. However, by late 1944, a massive backlog of undelivered mail—estimated at 17 million pieces—had accumulated in warehouses in Europe.

Recognizing the urgent need to address this issue, the U.S. Army sought to form a specialized unit capable of tackling the daunting task. The Women's Army Corps (WAC), already making strides in incorporating women into military roles, became the foundation for this effort.

The Heroic Legacy of the 6888th Battalion

Among the volunteers were African American women, eager to serve their country despite the segregation and discrimination they faced both within the military and society at large.

For many of these women, the decision to enlist was deeply personal. Some were motivated by patriotism, others by a desire to challenge racial and gender barriers, and still others by the promise of new opportunities and experiences. Their willingness to answer the call to serve, even under such challenging circumstances, demonstrated their resilience and commitment to making a difference.

Diversity and Unity: The Composition of the Six Triple Eight

The 6888th Battalion was composed predominantly of African American women, reflecting the military's segregation policies at the time. However, the unit also included women of Hispanic and Caribbean descent, making it one of the most diverse units in the military. This diversity became a source of strength for the battalion, as women from different backgrounds united to achieve a common goal.

The ages of the women in the Six Triple Eight ranged from 17 to 52, bringing together a mix of life experiences and perspectives. Some were young recruits eager for adventure, while others were seasoned professionals with backgrounds in education, nursing, and administration. Despite their differences, they shared a determination to prove their worth and contribute meaningfully to the war effort.

This sense of unity was fostered by the leadership of Major Charity Adams, who emphasized teamwork, discipline, and mutual respect. She recognized that the success of the battalion depended on its ability to work together, and she worked tirelessly to build a cohesive and supportive environment.

Training at Fort Oglethorpe: Facing Discrimination

Before deploying overseas, the women of the 6888th underwent rigorous training at Fort Oglethorpe in Georgia. Here, they learned the basics of military life, including combat readiness, gas mask drills, and physical fitness. However, their experience was far from typical, as they were forced to navigate the harsh realities of segregation and discrimination.

Fort Oglethorpe, like many military installations in the South, was governed by Jim Crow laws. The women were subjected to separate and unequal facilities, from dining halls to barracks, and were often treated with hostility by white soldiers and officers. Even within their own ranks, they faced challenges, as the military hierarchy often mirrored the racial inequalities of the broader society.

In addition to overt discrimination, the women had to contend with the skepticism of male officers who doubted their ability to perform their duties effectively. Crude remarks and dismissive attitudes were commonplace, but the women of the Six Triple Eight refused to be deterred.

To counter these challenges, the battalion developed a strong sense of camaraderie and resilience. They supported one another, drawing strength from their shared experiences and their belief in the importance of their mission. Under Major Adams' leadership, they remained focused on their training, determined to prove their capabilities and defy the prejudices that sought to undermine them.

Training at Fort Oglethorpe was both a test of their resolve and a preparation for the obstacles they would face overseas. By the time they completed their training, the women of the 6888th had forged a bond that would carry them through the trials ahead, ready to take on their historic mission in Europe.

The formation of the 6888th Battalion was a monumental achievement, not only in addressing a critical logistical need but also in challenging the systemic barriers that had long excluded African American women from meaningful roles in the military.

The call to serve, the diversity and unity within their ranks, and their perseverance through discrimination laid the groundwork for the success of the Six Triple Eight, setting the stage for their remarkable contributions to the war effort.

CHAPTER THREE

Mission Impossible: The Mail Backlog

The mission assigned to the 6888th Central Postal Directory Battalion was unlike anything the military had attempted before. With a backlog of over 17 million undelivered letters and packages piling up in European warehouses, the U.S. Army faced a morale crisis among its troops. Communication from home was vital for soldiers, providing emotional support and a sense of connection amidst the chaos of war.

The Six Triple Eight, led by Major Charity Adams, was tasked with tackling this monumental challenge. Despite adverse conditions and systemic discrimination, the battalion proved that what seemed impossible could be achieved through determination, innovation, and teamwork.

The Importance of Morale and Mail

In the midst of World War II, morale was a critical factor in sustaining the effectiveness of the armed forces. For soldiers stationed far from home, letters and care packages were lifelines, offering a sense of normalcy and hope. A simple letter from a loved one could provide comfort during the most harrowing moments, while a package from home might contain cherished items like photographs, baked goods, or small tokens of affection.

The Army understood this, encapsulating the significance of mail in the motto adopted by the 6888th: "No mail, low morale."

Without timely communication, soldiers' spirits could plummet, potentially affecting their performance on the battlefield. Mail not only strengthened the resolve of individual soldiers but also reinforced their ties to the home front, reminding them of what they were fighting for.

By late 1944, however, the military's postal system in Europe was overwhelmed. The sheer volume of mail generated by millions of troops, coupled with the logistical challenges of wartime operations, led to massive delays. Warehouses in England and France overflowed with unsorted letters and packages, many of which had been languishing for months.

The delays became a source of frustration and discontent among soldiers and their families, highlighting the urgent need for a solution.

The Daunting Task in Birmingham, England

When the 6888th arrived in Birmingham, England, in February 1945, they were greeted by a sight that underscored the enormity of their mission. Six warehouses, each the size of an aircraft hangar, were packed floor to ceiling with undelivered mail. The scale of the backlog was staggering: over 17 million letters and packages awaited sorting, with more arriving daily.

Complicating matters further were the poor conditions in which the mail was stored. Many packages contained perishable items like baked goods and homemade treats, which had long since spoiled. The smell of mildew and decay filled the air, and the warehouses were infested with scavenging rats. Sorting through the mess was not only an immense logistical challenge but also an unpleasant and sometimes hazardous task.

Adding to the difficulty was the constant threat of air raids. Birmingham, an industrial hub, was a frequent target for German bombers. The windows of the warehouses were painted black to prevent light from escaping and drawing the attention of enemy aircraft, forcing the women to work in dim, artificially lit conditions. This caused significant eye strain, further complicating their already demanding task.

Despite these obstacles, the women of the Six Triple Eight approached their mission with determination. Divided into three shifts, they worked around the clock, sorting mail seven days a week. Major Adams set clear goals and maintained high standards, emphasizing efficiency and accuracy.

The battalion's commitment to their mission inspired a collective sense of purpose, transforming what initially seemed like an insurmountable task into a manageable operation.

Logistics of Sorting 17 Million Letters

The process of sorting 17 million pieces of mail required a level of organization and efficiency rarely seen in military operations.

The Heroic Legacy of the 6888th Battalion

The women of the 6888th developed a meticulous system to handle the sheer volume of correspondence.

Each letter and package was checked against a directory of soldiers' names, which included information on their units and locations. Given the frequent movement of troops, this was no small feat; soldiers often changed locations or were transferred to different units, making accurate delivery a complex challenge.

The battalion maintained an extensive and constantly updated index of names, including duplicate or similar spellings, to ensure that every piece of mail reached its intended recipient. For example, they might have to differentiate between multiple soldiers named John Smith, each serving in a different branch or unit. The women displayed remarkable attention to detail, ensuring that even the most cryptic or incomplete addresses were deciphered.

To maintain efficiency, the women worked in assembly-line fashion, with each member assigned specific tasks. Some sorted mail by region or unit, while others focused on verifying addresses or updating the directory. The operation was streamlined to maximize output, and the battalion adhered to a strict schedule, working eight-hour shifts to ensure continuous progress.

Despite the adverse conditions, the women completed the task in just three months—half the time initially allotted. Their success not only restored morale among the troops but also demonstrated the capabilities of African American women in the military, challenging the prejudices and stereotypes that had long constrained their opportunities.

The Six Triple Eight's ability to overcome the challenges of the mail backlog in Birmingham was a testament to their resilience, ingenuity, and teamwork.

By tackling an unprecedented logistical problem under some of the most difficult conditions imaginable, they not only fulfilled a critical wartime need but also cemented their place in history as pioneers and problem-solvers. Their work in Birmingham set the stage for their next mission in France, proving that no task was beyond their reach.

CHAPTER FOUR

Challenges on Three Fronts

The 6888th Central Postal Directory Battalion faced more than logistical hurdles in their groundbreaking mission. The women of the Six Triple Eight contended with challenges on three fronts: systemic racism within the U.S. Army, pervasive misogyny in a male-dominated military structure, and the very real dangers of operating in a war zone. These adversities tested their resolve, unity, and determination, making their ultimate success all the more remarkable.

Fighting Racism Within the Army

Racism was entrenched in the U.S. Army during World War II, mirroring the segregation and discriminatory practices prevalent in American society at the time. The Women's Army Corps (WAC), though a progressive step toward inclusion, operated under the same segregationist policies as the rest of the military.

For the African American women of the 6888th, this meant facing not only the external pressures of war but also the internal challenges of institutionalized racism.

At Fort Oglethorpe, where the women trained, segregation was strictly enforced. African American soldiers were relegated to separate barracks, dining facilities, and recreational areas. They were often provided with inferior accommodations compared to their white counterparts. Despite their willingness to serve, these women were reminded at every turn that their contributions were undervalued.

When the Six Triple Eight arrived in Europe, they quickly realized that racism was not confined to American soil. The American Red Cross, tasked with providing support to troops overseas, denied Black WACs accommodations in its primary facilities, instead designating separate, substandard housing for them.

Major Charity Adams, refusing to accept this indignity, led a boycott of the Red Cross's segregated arrangements, ensuring her battalion upheld their dignity and unity.

Additionally, the women were often met with skepticism or outright hostility from white officers and soldiers. Many doubted their competence, questioning whether an all-Black, all-female battalion could handle such a critical mission. The women of the 6888th used these prejudices as fuel, proving their detractors wrong through their exceptional efficiency and professionalism.

Battling Misogyny in a Male-Dominated World

While racism was a pervasive challenge, misogyny posed an equally formidable obstacle for the women of the 6888th. The military, long dominated by men, was not designed to accommodate or support women, let alone women in leadership roles.

The very idea of women in uniform was met with skepticism, and female soldiers were often viewed as novelties or distractions rather than as essential contributors to the war effort.

Male officers frequently dismissed or undermined the women of the Six Triple Eight, doubting their ability to perform their duties. Some made lewd or inappropriate comments, reinforcing the perception that women did not belong in the military. Others imposed stricter standards on female soldiers, subjecting them to harsher scrutiny than their male counterparts.

Major Charity Adams faced these attitudes firsthand. As the first Black woman commissioned as an officer in the U.S.

Army, she bore the dual burden of representing both her race and her gender in an environment where neither was fully accepted. Despite the challenges, Adams commanded respect through her competence, poise, and unwavering commitment to her battalion. She set a powerful example for her subordinates, demonstrating that women could excel in leadership roles even in the face of systemic misogyny.

The women of the 6888th also supported one another, forming a tight-knit community that provided strength and encouragement. Together, they challenged the notion that women were unsuited for military service, paving the way for future generations of female soldiers.

The Heroic Legacy of the 6888th Battalion

Overcoming the Dangers of War

Beyond the challenges of racism and misogyny, the women of the Six Triple Eight faced the physical and emotional dangers inherent in operating in a war zone. Their deployment to Europe placed them squarely in the path of conflict, where the threat of air raids, harsh living conditions, and the psychological toll of war were constant realities.

Birmingham, England, where the battalion was initially stationed, had been heavily bombed during the Blitz and remained a target for German air attacks. The women worked in warehouses with windows painted black to avoid detection by enemy aircraft. The blackout conditions, while necessary for safety, made their already challenging work even more difficult, causing frequent eye strain and fatigue.

The cold, damp climate added another layer of hardship. The warehouses where they sorted mail were unheated, forcing the women to wear ski pants, field jackets, and gloves while working. Despite these measures, many suffered from illnesses caused by prolonged exposure to the harsh conditions.

The women also contended with the emotional toll of war. Sorting through millions of letters, they encountered firsthand the hopes, fears, and grief of soldiers and their families. Some packages contained reminders of soldiers who had died in combat, making their task a somber reminder of the war's human cost.

Yet, despite these challenges, the women of the 6888th persevered. Their commitment to their mission and to one another enabled them to overcome the dangers of war, ensuring that millions of soldiers received the vital morale boost that only a letter from home could provide.

The challenges faced by the 6888th Battalion were immense, spanning racism, misogyny, and the perils of war. Yet, these obstacles only strengthened their resolve. By confronting and overcoming adversity on multiple fronts, the women of the Six Triple Eight not only fulfilled their mission but also proved their strength, resilience, and value as soldiers.

Their success was a powerful testament to their courage and determination, laying the groundwork for greater inclusivity and recognition in the U.S. military.

CHAPTER FIVE

Life in Birmingham

The deployment of the 6888th Central Postal Directory Battalion to Birmingham, England, marked the beginning of their overseas journey. While their mission was defined by grueling work and high expectations, life in Birmingham revealed the layered complexities of their experience.

The women of the Six Triple Eight encountered not only the segregation they had hoped to leave behind but also harsh working conditions that tested their physical and emotional endurance. Yet, amid these challenges, they found ways to create moments of joy, connection, and community, highlighting their resilience and ability to thrive even in adversity.

Facing Segregation Overseas

For many members of the 6888th, serving in Europe brought the hope of escaping the overt racism they had faced in the United States. However, they quickly discovered that segregation and discrimination were not confined to American soil. While British society was less overtly racist than the Jim Crow laws of the U.S., the women still encountered prejudices perpetuated by the very institutions they served.

The American Red Cross, tasked with supporting U.S. troops overseas, denied the Black women of the Six Triple Eight accommodations in its main facilities.

Instead, they attempted to establish separate housing for the Black members of the Women's Army Corps. Major Charity Adams refused to accept such segregation and, with characteristic resolve, led a boycott of the Red Cross's segregated accommodations. Her leadership ensured that her battalion maintained their dignity and unity in the face of discrimination.

Interactions with their white American counterparts often highlighted the stark realities of segregation. Some white soldiers and officers refused to acknowledge the contributions of the 6888th, while others viewed them with suspicion or condescension. Despite these challenges, the women formed bonds with local British civilians, who often showed kindness and hospitality.

Many residents of Birmingham invited the women into their homes for Sunday dinners, providing a welcome respite from the discrimination they faced within their own ranks.

Harsh Working Conditions and Winter Struggles

The warehouses in Birmingham where the 6888th carried out their mission presented a host of physical challenges. Upon arrival, the women were greeted by six massive warehouses packed with undelivered mail. The facilities were cold, damp, and poorly lit, with no heating to protect against the harsh winter temperatures.

The women had to wear multiple layers of clothing, including ski pants and field jackets, just to keep warm as they worked.

The task itself was daunting. The warehouses were filled with packages containing spoiled food items like cakes and fried chicken, which had long since rotted. The smell of mildew and decay was pervasive, and rats scavenged among the piles of mail. The women worked in blackout conditions, with windows painted black to avoid drawing the attention of German bombers. This dim environment caused significant eye strain and made their work even more arduous.

The physical toll of the job was immense. Many women developed illnesses from the cold and damp conditions, while others suffered from exhaustion due to the long hours and demanding nature of the work. Yet, despite these challenges, the women of the 6888th remained focused on their mission, driven by their understanding of the importance of their task.

Moments of Joy: Bowling, Dancing, and Sunday Dinners

Amid the challenges of their work and the realities of wartime life, the women of the 6888th found ways to create moments of joy and maintain their morale. Social outings and leisure activities became essential for their well-being, providing opportunities to relax, bond, and reclaim a sense of normalcy.

In Birmingham, the women often ventured into the city during their off-hours. Bowling alleys became popular destinations, offering a chance to unwind and engage in friendly competition. Dancing was another favored pastime, with local venues hosting events where the women could socialize and enjoy music. These outings not only provided entertainment but also allowed the women to connect with the local community, many of whom welcomed them with open arms.

Sunday dinners with local families became cherished traditions. British residents, moved by the women's dedication and resilience, often invited members of the battalion into their homes. These meals offered a taste of home-cooked food and an opportunity to engage in meaningful cultural exchange. For the women of the 6888th, these moments of hospitality were a reminder of the kindness and humanity that persisted even in the midst of war.

Additionally, the women found ways to support one another within their unit. They celebrated birthdays, shared stories, and leaned on each other during difficult times. This sense of camaraderie was vital, fostering a strong sense of community that helped them navigate the challenges of their mission.

Life in Birmingham was a study in contrasts for the 6888th Battalion. They faced discrimination and grueling working conditions, yet they also experienced moments of joy, connection, and triumph.

The Heroic Legacy of the 6888th Battalion

Their ability to persevere and find light in even the darkest circumstances speaks to their extraordinary resilience and the bonds they formed as a unit. These experiences not only shaped their time in Birmingham but also cemented their legacy as trailblazers and role models for future generations.

CHAPTER SIX

Triumph in Adversity

The story of the 6888th Central Postal Directory Battalion is a testament to the power of perseverance and the triumph of the human spirit in the face of overwhelming odds. Despite grappling with discrimination, challenging working conditions, and the emotional toll of war, the women of the Six Triple Eight achieved remarkable feats.

Their success in completing their mission in record time and tackling an even greater challenge in France left an indelible mark on military history and established their legacy as pioneers of resilience and excellence.

The Heroic Legacy of the 6888th Battalion

Completing the Mission in Half the Time

When the 6888th Battalion arrived in Birmingham, England, they were met with a staggering sight: six massive warehouses overflowing with undelivered letters and packages destined for American soldiers stationed in Europe. The morale of the troops depended on their connection to loved ones back home, and the backlog threatened to sever this vital lifeline. Given a six-month deadline to clear the warehouses, the women of the Six Triple Eight set to work with unparalleled determination.

Operating in freezing, poorly lit warehouses, the battalion organized a grueling schedule of three eight-hour shifts that ran around the clock, ensuring continuous progress.

The task was monumental—not only did they have to sort and process the mail, but they also had to decipher incomplete or illegible addresses. Some letters were simply addressed to "Junior, somewhere in Europe" or "Johnny, U.S. Army." The women's ingenuity and resourcefulness enabled them to resolve these mysteries, ensuring that even the most obscurely addressed mail reached its intended recipient.

Within three months—half the allotted time—the battalion had sorted over 17 million pieces of mail. Their extraordinary efficiency and commitment not only restored communication between soldiers and their families but also showcased their capability and professionalism.

By completing the task in record time, the 6888th silenced their doubters and proved their indispensability to the war effort.

Moving to France: Tackling a Three-Year Mail Backlog

After their triumph in Birmingham, the women of the 6888th Battalion were redeployed to Rouen, France, in June 1945 to confront an even greater challenge. Here, they faced a staggering three-year accumulation of undelivered mail—millions of letters and packages that had languished in storage, awaiting processing. The conditions were no less challenging than those they had encountered in England.

Rouen, a city still bearing the scars of German occupation, offered limited infrastructure and resources. The warehouses were once again cold and poorly lit, and the backlog of mail was even more daunting. Despite these obstacles, the women of the 6888th approached their new assignment with the same determination and efficiency that had defined their work in Birmingham.

Working tirelessly in eight-hour shifts, they tackled the massive backlog with precision and speed. The women demonstrated a remarkable ability to adapt to new environments, utilizing their experience from Birmingham to streamline operations in Rouen. Within five months, they had cleared the backlog, achieving yet another extraordinary milestone.

The Heroic Legacy of the 6888th Battalion

By the time their work in France was complete, the war had ended in both the European and Pacific theaters. The battalion's mission was officially concluded, and the women of the Six Triple Eight began their journey back to the United States. Though they returned with little fanfare, their achievements resonated as a powerful testament to their skill, dedication, and resilience.

Legacy of Perseverance

The accomplishments of the 6888th Battalion went largely unrecognized in the years following World War II, overshadowed by the broader narratives of the war. However, their legacy as pioneers and trailblazers endured, serving as a source of inspiration for generations to come.

The Heroic Legacy of the 6888th Battalion

The women of the Six Triple Eight proved that African American women could excel in the military, challenging the prevailing stereotypes of the era. Their success in completing their mission demonstrated the value of diversity and inclusion, paving the way for greater opportunities for women and people of color in the armed forces.

Their perseverance in the face of adversity—whether confronting racism, misogyny, or the physical and emotional challenges of their work—set a powerful example of courage and determination. Major Charity Adams, in particular, emerged as a symbol of leadership and excellence, inspiring countless women to pursue careers in fields where they were underrepresented.

The Heroic Legacy of the 6888th Battalion

In March 2022, nearly 80 years after their service, the 6888th Battalion received the Congressional Gold Medal, one of the highest civilian honors in the United States. This long-overdue recognition highlighted the significance of their contributions and ensured their story would not be forgotten.

The legacy of the 6888th Battalion is a testament to the transformative power of perseverance. Their ability to triumph over adversity continues to inspire, reminding us of the strength and resilience that define true heroes. The women of the Six Triple Eight not only fulfilled their mission but also left a lasting imprint on history, proving that barriers can be broken and challenges overcome with determination and unity.

CHAPTER SEVEN

Overlooked and Forgotten

Despite their remarkable contributions to the war effort, the 6888th Central Postal Directory Battalion was largely overlooked in the years following World War II. Their success in clearing the mail backlog and boosting troop morale was a monumental achievement, yet the women of the Six Triple Eight returned to a society that failed to recognize their sacrifices and achievements.

This chapter explores the lack of recognition they faced, the unique challenges experienced by Black veterans upon their return, and how their stories were nearly erased from history.

The Lack of Recognition Post-War

When the 6888th Battalion returned to the United States in early 1946, their arrival was met with silence. Unlike the parades and celebrations held for other returning servicemen, there were no public ceremonies to honor their service. The women, who had worked tirelessly under difficult conditions, were quietly disbanded at Fort Dix, New Jersey, with little fanfare or acknowledgment of their accomplishments.

This lack of recognition was emblematic of the broader indifference toward Black veterans, particularly women, who had served during World War II.

The Heroic Legacy of the 6888th Battalion

The contributions of African Americans to the war effort were often minimized or ignored, a reflection of the pervasive racism and segregation that continued to define American society. For the women of the 6888th, this disregard was especially disheartening, given the extraordinary nature of their work and the obstacles they had overcome.

Adding to this oversight was the limited media coverage of the battalion's achievements. While other units were celebrated in newspapers and newsreels, the story of the Six Triple Eight was rarely told. The battalion's historic mission and groundbreaking leadership, exemplified by Major Charity Adams, remained largely unknown to the public for decades.

The Heroic Legacy of the 6888th Battalion

Challenges for Black Veterans Returning Home

The women of the 6888th Battalion, like many Black veterans, faced significant challenges upon their return to civilian life. Despite their service, they were met with the same systemic racism that had persisted before the war. The sacrifices they had made for their country did not shield them from discrimination in employment, housing, and public life.

The GI Bill, which provided educational and economic opportunities for returning servicemen, was often inaccessible to Black veterans due to discriminatory practices. Many institutions of higher learning refused to admit Black students, while banks and real estate agents denied loans and housing opportunities to African Americans. This systemic exclusion limited the ability of Black veterans to fully benefit from the post-war economic boom.

For the women of the 6888th, the intersection of race and gender presented additional challenges. As Black women, they faced discrimination not only from white society but also from male-dominated industries and institutions. Their military service, instead of being seen as a mark of achievement, was often dismissed or devalued.

Despite these obstacles, many members of the 6888th pursued higher education, professional careers, and community leadership roles. Major Charity Adams, for example, earned a master's degree from Ohio State University and went on to become a prominent educator and civic leader. Her determination to succeed in the face of adversity was a testament to the resilience and strength of the women of the 6888th Battalion.

Stories Lost to History

The achievements of the 6888th Battalion were not only overlooked but also nearly lost to history. For decades, their story remained untold, hidden in the archives and overshadowed by the broader narratives of World War II. The lack of documentation and recognition meant that the contributions of these trailblazing women were largely forgotten by subsequent generations.

The Heroic Legacy of the 6888th Battalion

This erasure was compounded by the limited efforts to preserve and share the stories of Black women who had served in the military. Historical accounts of World War II often centered on the experiences of white men, leaving little room for the narratives of African American women. As a result, the Six Triple Eight's groundbreaking achievements went uncelebrated for far too long.

The rediscovery of the 6888th Battalion's story in recent years has been driven by historians, archivists, and advocates committed to uncovering the hidden contributions of African Americans to American history. Oral histories, personal memoirs, and archival research have brought their story back into the public eye, ensuring that their legacy is no longer confined to the shadows.

In March 2022, nearly 80 years after their service, the women of the 6888th were awarded the Congressional Gold Medal, one of the highest civilian honors in the United States. This long-overdue recognition marked a significant step in correcting the historical record and honoring their contributions.

The post-war experience of the 6888th Battalion underscores the profound injustices faced by African American veterans and the enduring impact of systemic racism. Despite the lack of recognition and the challenges they encountered, the women of the Six Triple

Eight remained resilient, carving out their own paths and leaving a legacy of perseverance and courage.

Their story, once overlooked, now serves as a powerful reminder of the sacrifices and contributions of those who fought for a country that did not always fight for them.

CHAPTER EIGHT

Recognition at Last

The journey of the 6888th Central Postal Directory Battalion from obscurity to recognition is a testament to the enduring impact of their contributions. Despite decades of silence, their story was finally brought to light, culminating in one of the nation's highest honors.

This chapter explores the events and efforts that led to their recognition, the significance of their achievements being honored, and the long road to acknowledgment that spanned nearly eight decades.

President Biden's Congressional Medal of Honor

On March 14, 2022, President Joe Biden awarded the Congressional Gold Medal to the 6888th Central Postal Directory Battalion, a long-overdue recognition of their service during World War II. The ceremony, held in the nation's capital, was a historic moment not only for the women of the Six Triple Eight but also for the United States, which formally acknowledged their unparalleled contributions to the war effort.

The Congressional Gold Medal is one of the nation's highest civilian awards, reserved for individuals or groups who have made distinguished achievements and contributions. For the 6888th, this honor symbolized a reversal of decades of neglect and a validation of their hard work and perseverance.

During the ceremony, President Biden highlighted the significance of their service. He emphasized how their efficiency and determination had not only boosted morale for millions of American troops but also shattered barriers of race and gender. He acknowledged that their service came during a time of deep racial segregation, making their accomplishments even more extraordinary.

The medal was presented posthumously to the majority of the battalion's members, as only a few of the women were still alive to witness the historic moment. Fannie McClendon and Anna Mae Robertson, two surviving members, were honored in person, representing the battalion's spirit and resilience. The recognition by President Biden marked a pivotal moment in bringing their story to the forefront of American history.

Honoring the Six Triple Eight's Contributions

The Congressional Gold Medal ceremony was more than an event; it was a celebration of the 6888th's legacy and a public acknowledgment of their indispensable role in World War II. The achievements of the battalion were highlighted in speeches, documentaries, and exhibits that delved into their groundbreaking mission to clear the mail backlog in Europe.

The Heroic Legacy of the 6888th Battalion

This honor served as a platform to educate the public about the battalion's history and its broader implications. The women of the Six Triple Eight embodied the potential of African American women in the military, paving the way for future generations to serve with distinction.

The medal itself is a symbol of their hard-fought journey. On one side, the design features an image of the battalion working diligently in the mail warehouses, surrounded by their motto: "No Mail, Low Morale." The reverse side bears the words "Trailblazers in Service," emphasizing their role as pioneers.

In addition to the Congressional Gold Medal, local and national organizations have held events to honor the Six Triple Eight's contributions. Schools, museums, and veterans' associations have incorporated their story into curricula, exhibitions, and public programming, ensuring their legacy is preserved for generations to come.

The Long Road to Acknowledgment

The recognition of the 6888th Battalion did not happen overnight. For decades, their story remained untold, hidden in the margins of history. The journey to acknowledgment was driven by the tireless efforts of historians, advocates, and the families of the women who served.

One pivotal moment came with the publication of personal memoirs and oral histories, which provided firsthand accounts of the battalion's experiences. Major Charity Adams's memoir, One Woman's Army, offered a detailed account of her leadership and the challenges faced by the Six Triple Eight. These narratives helped bring their story to the attention of scholars and the public.

Advocates also played a critical role in ensuring the battalion received the recognition they deserved. Organizations like the National Association of Black Military Women and the Buffalo Soldier Educational and Historical Committee campaigned tirelessly for decades to highlight the contributions of African American women in the military. These efforts culminated in petitions, public awareness campaigns, and formal requests to Congress.

The Congressional Gold Medal ceremony was a watershed moment, but it also served as a reminder of the systemic neglect that had allowed the battalion's story to fade from memory. It underscored the importance of preserving and sharing the histories of marginalized groups, ensuring that their contributions are celebrated rather than forgotten.

The recognition of the 6888th Battalion marks a significant chapter in the ongoing effort to honor the contributions of African American women to American history. The Congressional Gold Medal and the renewed interest in their story reflect a growing commitment to inclusivity and historical justice.

While the road to acknowledgment was long and arduous, the recognition of the Six Triple Eight's achievements serves as a powerful reminder of their resilience, courage, and enduring legacy.

CHAPTER NINE

Charity Adams' Post-War Life

After the disbandment of the 6888th Central Postal Directory Battalion in 1946, Major Charity Adams, like many of the women she had led, faced the challenge of transitioning from military life to civilian life. Her post-war journey reflects her unrelenting drive, commitment to service, and dedication to advancing the cause of equality for African Americans, especially women.

This chapter delves into her educational achievements, personal life, community service, leadership roles, and her continued efforts to fight for equality in a post-war

America still deeply entrenched in racial and gender-based discrimination.

Education and Personal Life

One of the hallmarks of Charity Adams' post-war life was her pursuit of education and personal development. After her service in the 6888th, Adams took full advantage of the opportunities provided by the GI Bill, which enabled veterans to further their education. Despite the barriers of racism and sexism, Adams was determined to expand her knowledge and continue her academic pursuits.

In 1946, Adams enrolled at Ohio State University, where she earned a Master of Arts degree in Educational Psychology, marking another major achievement in her life.

This was particularly significant, as it was uncommon for African American women to attend graduate programs at the time, let alone excel within them. Adams's academic success was a testament to her tenacity and intellectual acumen, and it was part of her larger vision to serve her community through education.

Adams' commitment to learning and personal growth was also reflected in her strong work ethic and integrity. During her time at Ohio State, she demonstrated leadership qualities that would continue to define her career and community involvement.

Her academic achievements, coupled with her military service, solidified her reputation as a trailblazer, a position she embraced with grace and determination.

In addition to her educational pursuits, Adams' personal life took an important step forward in 1949 when she married Stanley A. Earley Jr., a medical student whom she had met during her time in the military. Their marriage was not only a personal milestone but also marked a deepening of Adams' commitment to family and community. The couple eventually settled in Dayton, Ohio, where Adams would continue her work both in the educational sector and as a civic leader.

Community Service and Leadership

Charity Adams' passion for education and her sense of responsibility toward the well-being of others translated into a life dedicated to community service and leadership. Upon settling in Dayton, Adams became a prominent figure in both local and national organizations, working tirelessly to improve the lives of African Americans and women.

One of her most significant contributions was the founding of the Black Leadership Development Program, which she established to provide education, training, and mentorship for African American youth. The program aimed to empower young people by helping them navigate the barriers posed by racism and offering them the tools to succeed in higher education and professional careers. This initiative reflected Adams' lifelong belief in the transformative power of education and her desire to build a legacy of empowerment for African Americans.

In addition to her work with the Black Leadership Development Program, Adams was also actively involved in the American Red Cross. She served on the board of the local chapter in Dayton, where she worked to address the needs of marginalized communities. Through this role, Adams was able to bridge the gap between her military experience, her commitment to public service, and her dedication to community-building.

Adams' leadership extended beyond the local level as well. She was an active member of several national organizations focused on racial equality, women's rights, and military veterans. She used her platform and influence to advocate for the rights and recognition of African American veterans, ensuring their stories were heard and their contributions acknowledged.

Her civic engagement was not only a reflection of her personal values but also of her broader vision for social change. Adams understood that true progress could only be made by fighting for systemic reforms that would benefit future generations, particularly those who had been historically marginalized.

Her leadership, both in her professional life and within her community, was an extension of the resilience and determination she had shown as the commanding officer of the 6888th Battalion.

Continuing the Fight for Equality

Even after her formal retirement from military service, Charity Adams did not stop fighting for justice. Her life after the war was defined by an unrelenting commitment to the causes of racial and gender equality. In an era when both African Americans and women faced substantial obstacles in nearly every facet of public life, Adams used her platform to advocate for those who were often overlooked or excluded.

Adams's involvement in national organizations like the National Council of Negro Women and the National Association of Colored Women's Clubs allowed her to continue her activism on a larger scale. She was a strong advocate for racial equality and women's rights, addressing the need for both African American and female representation in positions of power. She argued passionately for the equal treatment of African American veterans, many of whom, like herself, had been overlooked or dismissed after their service.

In addition to her work on behalf of veterans, Adams was a staunch supporter of the civil rights movement, understanding that the fight for racial equality extended far beyond the battlefields of World War II.

She saw the need for long-term, systemic change, and she continued to speak out against discrimination in all its forms. Adams's legacy as a leader was inextricably linked to her commitment to social justice and her belief that equality was a right, not a privilege.

Her advocacy extended to her personal life as well. As a wife, mother, and grandmother, Adams sought to create an environment of understanding and support for her family. Her commitment to her family was a natural extension of her larger commitment to community, and she encouraged the younger generations to continue her work for equality.

The Heroic Legacy of the 6888th Battalion

Charity Adams' post-war life was marked by a profound sense of duty and a dedication to improving the lives of others. Through her education, community service, and unwavering fight for equality, Adams made an indelible mark on American society. Her legacy as a trailblazer, both in the military and in civilian life, is a testament to her resilience, intelligence, and tireless commitment to justice.

Major Charity Adams' post-war life exemplified the qualities that defined her leadership: courage, perseverance, and an unyielding desire to make a difference in the world.

CHAPTER TEN

The Six Triple Eight in Modern Memory

The legacy of the 6888th Central Postal Directory Battalion, though overlooked for much of the 20th century, has experienced a powerful resurgence in recent years, fueled by renewed interest in the group's remarkable story.

From the cultural impact of Tyler Perry's film The Six Triple Eight to the personal stories of surviving veterans, the recognition of the battalion's achievements has transformed them from unsung heroes to celebrated icons of resilience and trailblazing leadership.

This chapter explores how the 6888th has been remembered and honored in contemporary times, particularly through modern media, the voices of surviving veterans, and the battalion's lasting significance in the contexts of Black history and women's rights.

Tyler Perry's Film and Its Cultural Impact

In 2024, The Six Triple Eight, a film written and directed by Tyler Perry, brought the incredible story of the 6888th Battalion to a new generation, creating a cultural moment that has amplified their contributions to World War II and American history.

Starring Kerry Washington as Major Charity Adams, the film captures the emotional and historical significance of the battalion's service, as well as the deeply personal struggles of these women of color who fought not only against the adversities of war but also against racial and gender-based discrimination.

Tyler Perry's involvement in the project added another layer of depth to the film's impact. Known for his long history of producing films that center on Black lives, culture, and history, Perry took on The Six Triple Eight with a deep respect for the individuals whose stories had long been forgotten.

Perry's commitment to telling stories that empower and uplift marginalized communities is evident in his careful approach to the film, ensuring that the battalion's sacrifices and contributions were portrayed authentically and respectfully.

The film's release in select theaters and subsequent streaming on Netflix has had a profound effect on raising awareness about the 6888th. It has introduced the battalion's incredible story to millions of viewers worldwide and sparked important conversations about the history of Black women in the military, the roles women played during World War II, and the overlooked contributions of African American veterans.

The emotional resonance of the film, paired with Perry's star-studded cast, has contributed to the battalion's resurgence in modern memory, providing the recognition that these women had long been denied.

In addition to its entertainment value, The Six Triple Eight has served as an educational tool, inspiring people of all ages to learn more about the battalion and their place in history. The film highlights the importance of historical storytelling in shaping collective memory and has paved the way for future projects that explore untold or overlooked aspects of Black and women's history.

Veterans' Stories: Fannie McClendon, Anna Mae Robertson, and Lena Derriecott King

While much of the 6888th Battalion's story was kept in the shadows for decades, the personal testimonies of surviving veterans have played an essential role in bringing their legacy into the public consciousness. Veterans like Fannie McClendon, Anna Mae Robertson, and Lena Derriecott King represent the living history of the battalion, and their stories have provided critical insight into the experiences of these pioneering women.

Fannie McClendon, one of the few surviving veterans of the battalion, has spoken about her time in the 6888th with pride and poignancy. McClendon's recollections serve as a vital source of first-hand history, offering a window into the struggles and triumphs of the battalion.

In interviews, McClendon has shared how the battalion's dedication to completing their mission against all odds, despite the overwhelming challenges they faced, left an indelible mark on her life. Her stories, shared in interviews and articles, have become a key part of the battalion's modern memory.

Similarly, Anna Mae Robertson, who, like McClendon, served in the 6888th, has become a key figure in preserving the legacy of the battalion. As one of the last remaining veterans, Robertson has attended events and shared her experiences at various forums, helping to bridge the gap between history and contemporary understanding.

Robertson's firsthand accounts of the battalion's experiences during the war have helped give voice to those who were once forgotten, ensuring that their legacy is preserved for future generations.

Perhaps most impactful in the recent resurgence of interest in the battalion's story is Lena Derriecott King, whose meeting with Tyler Perry in April 2022 inspired him to make The Six Triple Eight. Before her passing in January 2024 at the age of 100, King's involvement in the film project allowed her to witness firsthand the recognition of her service.

In an emotional Instagram video, Perry shared the profound experience of watching the unfinished film with King just prior to her death.

King's tears and gratitude were a testament to the emotional weight of the story, which for so long had been kept in the shadows. In her final years, King's legacy, alongside the stories of other veterans, cemented the 6888th's place in history as a symbol of courage, resilience, and pride.

The stories of these veterans continue to resonate deeply with audiences, providing living testimony to the 6888th's enduring legacy. They have become spokespeople for the battalion's history, ensuring that their voices remain a central part of the cultural narrative surrounding the 6888th.

The 6888th's Place in Black and Women's History

The 6888th Battalion's significance extends far beyond its military accomplishments. It represents a pivotal moment in the fight for both racial and gender equality. For African American women, the 6888th served as a groundbreaking example of what was possible even in the face of systemic racism and sexism. The women of the 6888th not only broke racial barriers but also challenged the prevailing norms of what women—especially Black women—could achieve in the military.

Their story is woven into the broader tapestry of Black history, particularly during a time when the Civil Rights Movement had not yet gained widespread momentum.

The Heroic Legacy of the 6888th Battalion

The battalion's courage and determination provided a shining example of the untold contributions of African Americans during World War II. Their service was a precursor to the larger societal shifts that would take place in the 1950s and 1960s, as Black veterans, activists, and citizens began to demand recognition and equality.

In the context of women's history, the 6888th represents a watershed moment in the fight for women's rights, particularly for women of color. At a time when women were often relegated to support roles or excluded from active combat, the members of the 6888th took on a vital mission in the heart of a war zone.

The Heroic Legacy of the 6888th Battalion

Their work helped bolster morale for American troops, proving that women—regardless of race—could perform essential and demanding tasks just as effectively as their male counterparts. The recognition of their role in World War II adds to the rich history of women's contributions to the military and society at large.

The 6888th's place in both Black and women's history continues to grow, especially as more people learn about their story through films, books, and media coverage. Their legacy has paved the way for future generations of women, particularly Black women, to pursue careers in the military and other fields that were once closed to them.

The Heroic Legacy of the 6888th Battalion

The battalion's story is a testament to the indomitable spirit of women who defied societal expectations and, through their resilience, changed the course of history.

The 6888th's place in modern memory underscores the importance of acknowledging and celebrating the contributions of those who have been overlooked in the past.

The resurgence of interest in their story is a powerful reminder that history is constantly being rewritten, and that the voices of those who were marginalized for so long deserve to be heard. Their contributions are not only important for the historical record but also serve as an inspiration to future generations of women and people of color striving to make their mark on the world.

The 6888th Central Postal Directory Battalion's remarkable journey—from its inception during World War II to its resurgence in modern memory—reflects the strength, perseverance, and resilience of the women who served. Their legacy, though delayed in recognition, now occupies an essential place in both Black history and women's history, inspiring all who learn about their incredible achievements.

The cultural impact of their story—amplified by Tyler Perry's film, the voices of surviving veterans, and the battalion's recognition in recent years—ensures that the 6888th's place in history will never be forgotten.

CONCLUSION

The Legacy of Major Charity Adams and the 6888th Battalion

The story of Major Charity Adams and the 6888th Central Postal Directory Battalion is one of profound courage, determination, and resilience in the face of immense adversity. It is a legacy that not only celebrates the strength and fortitude of these pioneering women but also highlights their critical contributions to the war effort during World War II.

Despite the systemic racism, gender discrimination, and physical hardships they faced, the women of the 6888th proved that they could accomplish what many thought was impossible. Their story, though long overlooked, is a testament to the power of perseverance and unity.

At the forefront of this battalion's efforts was Major Charity Adams, a trailblazer who shattered racial and gender barriers to become the first African American woman to lead a U.S. Army unit during wartime. Under her leadership, the 6888th not only successfully completed the overwhelming task of sorting millions of letters and parcels but did so with remarkable efficiency, finishing the mission in half the expected time.

Adams's steadfast commitment to her soldiers, her refusal to accept segregation, and her determination to uphold the dignity and humanity of every member of her battalion remain at the heart of their enduring legacy.

The 6888th's mission—sorting the backlog of mail for American soldiers stationed abroad—may seem like a logistical task, but the emotional significance of their work cannot be overstated. For the soldiers on the front lines, receiving mail from home was often the only connection to a world beyond the war.

The battalion's success in delivering that connection, despite facing horrific working conditions, segregation, and constant dangers from the war, was an act of profound empathy and service. They gave the soldiers hope when it was most needed, proving that even in the darkest times, small acts of kindness and service could make all the difference.

Lessons of Courage, Unity, and Perseverance

The legacy of the 6888th Battalion offers profound lessons on courage, unity, and perseverance. These women faced obstacles that would have overwhelmed many, yet they persevered. They proved that courage is not the absence of fear, but the determination to act despite it.

Their decision to push through segregated conditions, to fight against the limits placed on them due to their gender and race, and to complete a task that seemed insurmountable speaks to their inner strength and resilience.

The Heroic Legacy of the 6888th Battalion

Perhaps the most powerful lesson from the 6888th's story is the power of unity in the face of adversity. Though these women came from different backgrounds and cultures—African American, Hispanic, Caribbean—they stood together with a common goal: to serve their country and uplift one another.

The battalion's success was built on their collective spirit, as they supported each other in the face of harsh working conditions, physical exhaustion, and the pervasive racism that existed both within and outside the military. Their ability to set aside their individual differences and work as a cohesive unit is a powerful reminder of the strength that comes from solidarity, especially in moments of crisis.

Additionally, their perseverance in the face of overwhelming challenges offers a timeless lesson. The women of the 6888th not only completed their mission but did so faster and more efficiently than anticipated. Their accomplishments reflect the profound impact of determination, dedication, and a refusal to accept defeat. Their story proves that even the most daunting tasks are achievable when there is a collective will to succeed.

Inspiring Future Generations to Overcome Adversity

The story of the 6888th is one that resonates deeply with contemporary struggles, providing a powerful example for future generations. In an era where issues of racial and gender inequality still persist, the bravery and resilience of the women in the 6888th offer both inspiration and a blueprint for overcoming adversity.

For young women, especially women of color, the example set by Major Charity Adams and the members of the 6888th serves as a reminder that barriers can be broken, no matter how daunting they may seem.

Their ability to serve their country at a time when few women—let alone women of color—were given the opportunity to do so speaks to the potential within every individual to defy societal expectations and change the course of history. The 6888th's legacy offers a powerful example that women can lead, they can fight, and they can achieve greatness, regardless of the obstacles placed in their path.

Moreover, the story of the 6888th resonates with anyone who faces hardship or exclusion. It serves as a reminder that perseverance, even in the face of systemic challenges, is crucial to creating lasting change. The women of the 6888th embodied resilience in the truest sense, not only enduring but thriving in the most difficult of circumstances.

Their story serves as a beacon of hope for those who face adversity today, showing that persistence, hard work, and an unwavering belief in one's mission can turn the tide against seemingly insurmountable challenges.

The contributions of the 6888th also offer a crucial lesson in the importance of collective action and solidarity. The unity of the battalion, despite the challenges they faced, is a testament to the strength that comes from working together toward a common goal. The lessons of courage, unity, and perseverance they impart are just as relevant today as they were during World War II.

Ultimately, the heroic legacy of Major Charity Adams and the 6888th Battalion proves that history is often made by those whose contributions are overlooked or marginalized.

It is only through the collective efforts of individuals like the women of the 6888th that we can truly appreciate the impact of courage, unity, and perseverance in shaping history. By honoring their legacy, we are reminded of the power within all of us to overcome adversity and to leave a lasting mark on the world.

As we move forward, it is imperative that the story of the 6888th Battalion and the remarkable women who served within it continue to be shared, celebrated, and honored. Their courage and resilience are an enduring source of inspiration, a powerful reminder that no matter the obstacles, we all have the capacity to make a difference.

Their legacy is a call to action for future generations to continue the fight for equality, justice, and the recognition of all those who have been forgotten by history. Through their example, we are reminded that in the face of adversity, there is always the possibility for triumph.

THANKS FOR READING!!!